The Aviary

ILLUSTRATED BY CLAIRE SCULLY AND RICHARD MERRITT

• EDITED BY SOPHIE SCHREY • DESIGNED BY JACK CLUCAS • COVER DESIGN BY JOHN BIGWOOD •

The birds in this book appear in the following order:

Atlantic puffin • barn swallows • Indian peafowl • macaw • grey crowned crane • bald eagle
swallow-tailed hummingbird • mallard ducks • brown pelican • Welsummer chicken • lovebirds
southern cassowary • South American great horned owl • red-billed toucan • swan • blue jay
emperor penguin chick • Victoria crowned pigeon • greater flamingo • Queen Victoria's riflebird • raven
white-capped albatross • common kingfisher • common ostrich • great blue herons • Major Mitchell's cockatoo
long-legged buzzard • red-bellied woodpecker • hoopoe • pheasant • blue-footed boobies

First edition for North America published in 2016
by Barron's Educational Series, Inc.

First published in Great Britain in 2016 by LOM ART, an imprint of
Michael O'Mara Books Limited, 9 Lion Yard, Tremadoc Road, London SW4 7NQ

All inquiries should be addressed to:
Barron's Educational Series, Inc.
250 Wireless Boulevard
Hauppauge, NY 11788
www.barronseduc.com

ISBN: 978-1-4380-0895-0

Printed in China

9 8 7 6 5 4 3 2

BARRON'S

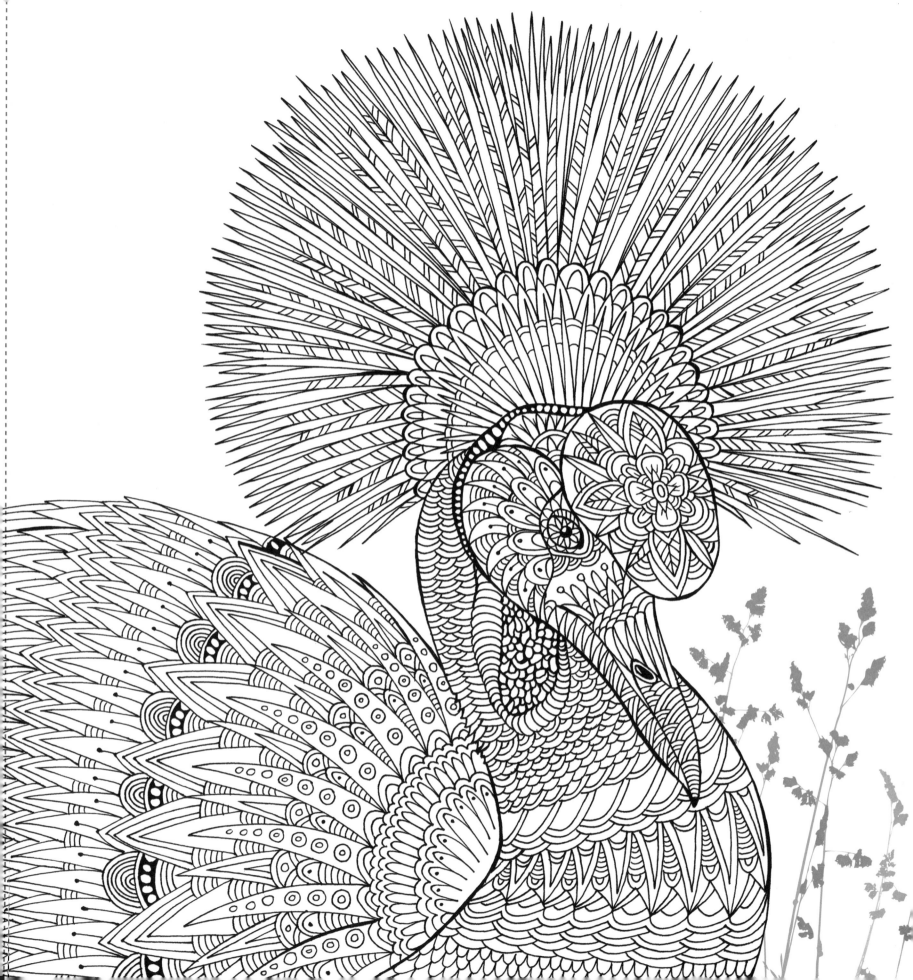

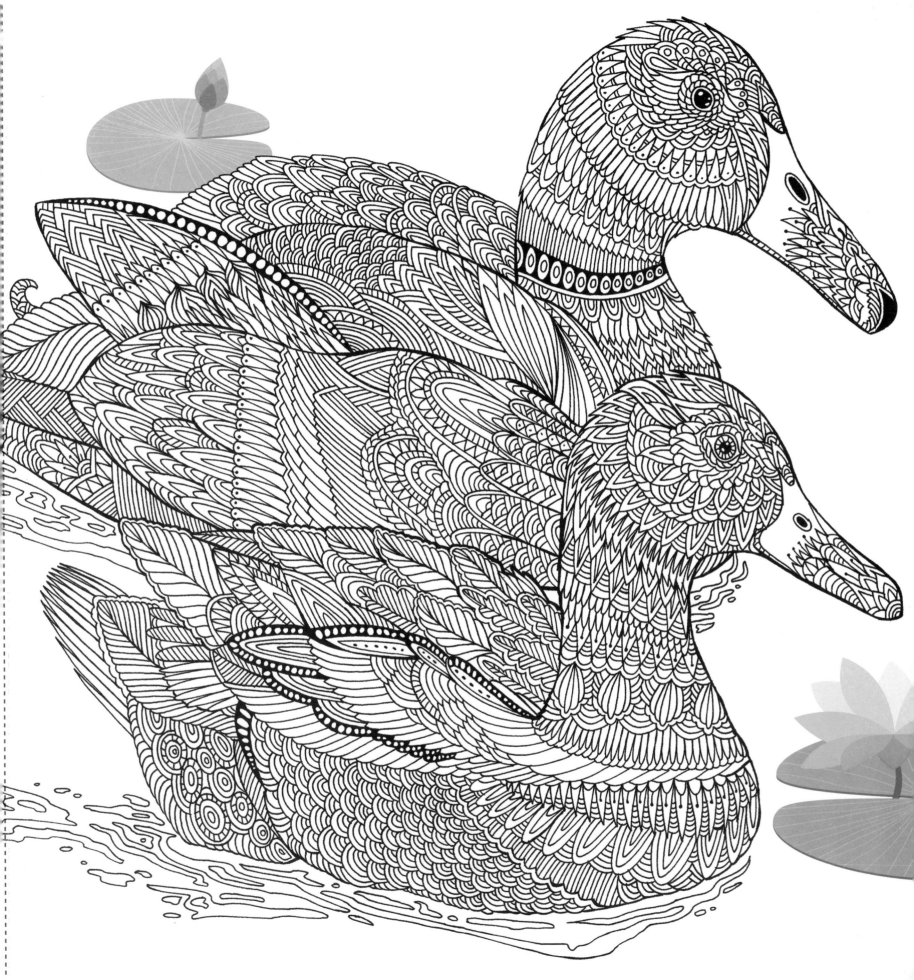